A
COUNTRY
BOOK OF DAYS

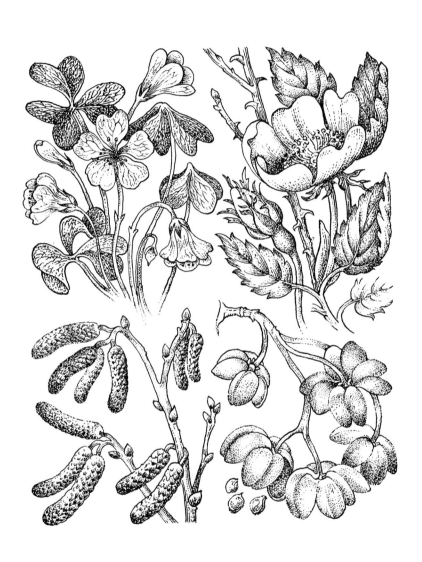

A
Country
Book of Days

HEATHER &
ROBIN TANNER

The Old Stile Press

First published in 1986 by The Old Stile Press

Published in this edition in 1988
by Impact Books, 112 Bolingbroke Grove,
London SW11 1DA

British Library Cataloguing in Publication Data
Tanner, Heather
    A country book of days.
    1. British calendar customs
    I. Title II. Tanner, Robin, *1904–*
    394.2'6941

ISBN 0-245-54687-1

Printed and bound in Great Britain
by Richard Clay Ltd., Chichester, Sussex

FOREWORD

The Day must be our earliest unit of time, evolved with the planet. All things obey the rhythm of light and dark: the very rocks expand in midday heat and cool with nightfall. No wonder early Man worshipped the sun, moon a close second, waxing and waning with sinister power over more than the tides. He knew dawn, midday, dusk, but the artificial 'hour' had to await the invention of a timepiece. Why twenty-four? Why sixty minutes? Did each of sixty seconds measure a heartbeat? Now seasons—summer and winter solstice, spring and autumn equinox—demanded observance, if only for food, and of their inevitable recurrence was born the reckoning of the years. The rhythms were in the blood, birth and death, to be celebrated and exorcised, and though Christianity tried to put a stop to the heathen junketings, ingeniously providing a saint for each festival, and then more to fill up the year, nature survived nurture. ¶ 'A calendar! a calendar! find out moonshine!' cry Shakespeare's rustic actors. Was the Zodiac the earliest, arbitrarily linking the months with astrology, which willing suspension of disbelief can bring back to fashion? Today, looking 'with forward and reverted eyes', no ordered life can be led without almanac or diary, to be punctuated with the inexorably approaching event, dreaded or welcomed. Some of us subconsciously evolve our own visual

7

charts. E. F. Schumacher saw numbers 'in a specific pattern curving out into space', and was with difficulty persuaded that this was not the general experience. I myself could not keep a Friday-in-July appointment without seeing it ensconced on the fifth day of a week (white, Saturday and Sunday being black and raised like piano keys) at the zenith of a semi-circular twelvemonth. Here then are our twenty-six selected days that will recur, with additional enriching anniversaries, in the chain of semi-circles stretching away to infinity.

CONTENTS

NEW YEAR'S DAY

The two-headed god Janus does not look back for long. Ungratefully the old year is soon forgotten, Christmas decorations are packed away, and after the full stop one can start afresh with a capital letter, making New Year resolutions which once broken can also be thankfully set aside. ¶ Winter may have been mild so far, but 'January brings the snow', and with it the irrational longing for some sign of Spring. Snowdrop spears may have been here before the first flakes fell, but the first aconite's little hoop, the colour of earth, can escape unnoticed. Its brave progress can be packed into a haiku:

Staple first thrusts through;
Then gold cup, green-fringed saucer
Faith in Spring renew.

H.T.

II

PLOUGH MONDAY

Plough Monday was the first Monday after New Year's Day, celebrated by the procession of a festively decorated plough throughout the village or town. As a symbol of life, wresting from the earth man's staple food, it was a kind of god. And even though it has progressed from simple breastplough, little more than a huge spade, to horse-drawn (or oxen-drawn, as some can still remember) and now to tractor, the craft is still kept alive in ploughing matches, with horse as well as by machinery. It is commemorated in inn signs (it must be one of the commonest), in inscriptions on old mugs, and in metaphor: to plough through a task, to plough a lonely furrow; ploughed in an examination. The very word, originally ending in a guttural sound, suggests the arduousness of the work, and weary indeed must have been the ploughman—and his horse!—as he plodded his homeward way.

¶ No one wants to put that clock back.

CANDLEMAS: February 2nd

The 'Purification' of the B.V.M. has been adapted to thanksgiving for a safe delivery, a good reason for a candle-lit procession, the still waxen flames transforming the wearers of scarlet cassocks and white surplices to a communion of saints. ¶ In the drawing are a tall smith-wrought standard 'lamp', a Jewish candle-stand with Star of David and 'server' that lighted the eight branches. And 'here comes the candle to light you to bed', a brass one with firm thumb-grip, set ever-ready on the mantlepiece; and here in rose-painted china one of a pair, last possessions of an ancestor descended from four-storey town house to one small room. ¶ Those of us for whom candles were essential household gear will remember the tallow running down the pristine surface, the acrid smell as the flame was snuffed out, candle-made shadow pictures on the wall, the waits' candled lanterns for their round of carol-singing on Christmas Eve, and next morning, hung from the brass bedstead, a stocking with bulges to be explored by candle-light.

15

ST. VALENTINE'S DAY: February 14th

Old lady whom I never knew, your Valentine I wear,
Though in the manifold bequests I was not named an heir.

No customary kith and kin with your departing breath
Assumed control: neighbour it was inherited your death.

His care no curious eye should scan incriminating page,
Nor as senility dismiss your struggles with old age.

Thus he found the unclaimed brooch asking to be mine—
An onyx fashioned as a heart, sent as a Valentine.

No kith or kin? A loving friend has acted a son's part,
Bidding you goodbye, while I, a daughter, wear your heart.

H.T.

To my Dear Acquaintance ♡

Oh write to me where'er thou be, One little line if but to tell That thou art happy Thou art well. ♡ ♡ ♡

17

MOTHERING SUNDAY

Commerce has now crudely revived a custom happily dying a natural death. This was the one day off, mid-Lent, vouchsafed to the servants of 'big houses' for visiting the parents some had left while mere children. From their meagre wages, most sent home, they could afford no gift for the occasion, but brought a posy of white and blue violets, while Mother made 'furmity' for a treat. The word is 'frumenty' (French 'froment', wheat), but Wessex speech likes to curl the 'r' round the tongue. ¶ Hardy calls the 'concoction' 'antiquated slop', and the future Mayor of Casterbridge had never tasted it before that fatal night when, having had too much, heavily laced with rum, he sold his wife; but it is still made locally on Mothering Sunday. It is a delicious milk pudding of hulled wheat, with currants and sultanas previously 'plimmed up', and sugar and spice to taste, thickened with flour or, better, a final enrichment of eggs. The wheat must first be soaked for three days, the water changed daily, then cooked in water for two or three hours till the grains are soft and bursting.

Bon appétit!

R. (from telephone). *They can't come. Car trouble.*

H. Ram in the thicket! I needn't cook now.

R. *Let's celebrate—do something worthwhile!*

H. The stair-carpet!

R. *What's wrong with the stair-carpet?*

H. Tread never changed! Moth. Woodworm.

R. *We'll go out . I want to draw a good ash tree.*

H. Very well. You lock up while I tidy.

R. (hunting wildly). *Where's the key?*

H. In the usual place. *(Produces it.)*

R. *It wasn't there five minutes ago.*

   (Half an hour elapses, H. still tidying.)

H. Suppose the postman brings a parcel?

R. *If we wait we shall start answering letters.*

H. Don't go out in hopes of hurrying me—it's
   paralysing. You'll need Wellingtons.

R. (one foot in). *Ugh! They've watered plants over them!*

H. I never water them.

R. *Then you should . . . Why that bag?*

H. (pocketing it). In case we find litter.

R. *I'm not going a-littering: I'm drawing. Are you wearing the
   right glasses?*

H. No. But where are they? *(Both search. Postman knocks.)*

R. (staggering in with post). *Raining cats and dogs!*

21

EASTER DAY

Eostre, goddess of the east, of dawn, of Spring equinox, goes back to Indo-European roots: Sanskrit has the equivalent word. 'Easter month' was the Anglo-Saxons' name for the second month of their year. Christianity most fittingly turned it into the festival of Resurrection, and with Wycliffe's Bible (1389) a new word 'pascha', from the Hebrew passover, was also used for Easter. It survives in Northumbria, where children dye their 'pace' eggs, wrapped in onion skins and hardboiled, in chance patterns of rich browns and golds, and roll them about till they break and can be eaten. ¶ Easter egg celebration, like the Christmas tree, is of German origin: real eggs hand-painted, resist-dyed and drawn-on, and then eggs of chocolate, of metal, marble, wood, and of cardboard covered with bright scraps and lined with pretty sprigged paper, fitting one inside the other like Russian dolls. Yet nothing is more beautiful than the egg of wild bird, enchantingly varied in colours and markings, or, brown or white, of free-range hen—mathematically functional in shape, designed to slip from the bird, not to roll over ledges, to nestle in soft feathers or in the hollow of the hand, symbol of continuing new life.

23

...never came so sweet? To show how costly summer was at hand...

If the date of Shakespeare's birthday, April 23rd, were not one of the very few facts known of him, he could have been allocated an April birthday—how he loved the very word!

> *...proud-pied April dressed in all his trim*
> *Hath put a spirit of youth in everything,*

And how he celebrated April flowers!

> *When daisies pied and violets blue*
> *And lady-smocks all silver white*
> *And cuckoo-buds of yellow hue*
> *Do paint the meadows with delight.*

Any spring flower was called cuckoo: those cuckoo-buds were marsh marigolds, the 'winking mary-buds' that 'oped their golden eyes' in the Avon-bordered pastures of his home. ¶ For although Shakespeare was no botanist, and like blind Milton could take poet's licence with the seasons, mingling the 'nodding violet' with sweet musk roses and eglantine, he noted the ruby spots in the gold coats of cowslips and the varying colour of heartsease, 'before milkwhite, now purple with love's wound.' Today, grown conservation-wise, he would have sung of the speedwell's 'darling blue' and Jack-in-the-hedge's swiftly ascending spires of little white crosses.

24

MAY DAY

'Cast not a clout till May be out' is disputed every year: is it the end of the month that is meant, or hawthorn blossom? It comes to the same thing, for may is seldom to be seen when lasses and lads crown their May Queen and dance round the maypole. All too often it is blackthorn that 'starreth now his bough on the eve of May.' But if Spring comes late it seems over-eager to make up for lost time, with cowslip — dandelion — buttercup in swift spendthrift succession. May Morris implies this transience in embroidered lettering at Walthamstow Museum:

> *Yet the wise say*
> *that not unblest he dies*
> *who has known a single May day.*

Birdsong too accelerates: the chorus crescendoes till sleep is impossible after dawn:

> *The innocent turtledove says all there is to say;*
> *Cuckoo and barefaced jay,*
> *Indolent blackbird in his rich articulate way,*
> *Chiffchaff and great tit ticking monotonously all day.*
> *Every bird in the wood, the harsh and sweet,*
> *Has his poetry complete:*
> *There is no more to say.*

R.T.

26

We were in south-west France, not alpine nor garigue nor château country, but gently undulating agricultural landscape, with nightingales and golden orioles calling unseen, and hoopoes descending from their orchards to pitch on the road ahead. Yet wherever we halted, to consult the map, to admire a view or to eat a picnic lunch, we would find some rare flower as it were laid on for us—adonis, bastard balm, blue pimpernel, or the fantastic squiggle of lizard orchid beside the narrow lanes meandering from flowerpot-tiled farm to farm. ¶ One day at the edge of a field of young wheat we were arrested by two plants scarcely six feet apart. One we recognised as wild gladiolus, though recognise is hardly the word, so different was this mobile slender plant, its rich red petals elegantly narrow, from the unyielding outsize ramrod forced earthwards in the flower-arranger's vase. The other was utterly unfamiliar. Orchid? Not quite. But if not, what? The brown petals seemed to wrap the stem, the conspicuous dark tongue wriggling from a closed 'helmet', as if a lizard orchid had crossed with the white helleborine, that refuses to open. We had to consult the flora. . . . It was long-tongued serapias. And what made the day even more red-letter was seeing as we hunted how many more extraordinary flowers remained to be found.

OAKAPPLE DAY: May 29th

'Show your oak! Show your oak!' cried the Big Girl on arriving at school on the 29th of May, flourishing a twig with a fat squeezable pink-flushed oakapple. Without oak we could have been stung with nettles—just like children to keep up a rule permitting a little cruelty. Anyway we younger ones were automatically royalist, wanting to be princesses when we grew up, though all we knew of Charles was the story that he had hid in an oak while his enemies passed unwittingly below him. We did know that the 'apple' was none, having cut the pincushion in two and found the grub. A good opportunity for 'Our Governess', had her omniscience extended to gall wasps, to give us a Nature Study lesson. ¶ The Opies' distribution map shows very few places south of Worcester (Cromwell's victory) where the custom survives. In Great Wishford (South Wiltshire) the day commemorates not Charles but the proclamation on March 15th 1603 of the villagers' right 'by ancient custom and time out of mind' to collect firewood in Grovelly Forest. In 1892 an Oak Apple Club was founded to ensure the perpetuation of this once movable feast on May 29th—
the very date on a brass of 1473
in their church.

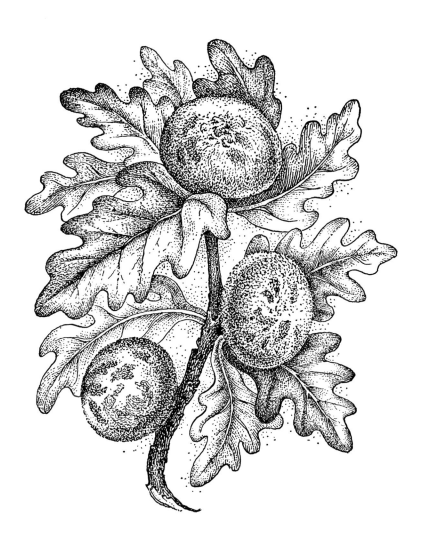

31

WELL-DRESSING: June or July

Was it not from water that covers three-quarters of our planet that we ourselves evolved, our bodies still largely composed of water? Haunted by films of women scratching for desert water, to be carried home mile after baking mile, or of Pacific islanders poisoned by drinking the undrinkable now contaminating our own seas, can we wonder that the mysterious sources of water were once worshipped with ritual? Well-dressing, in the few places where it still survives, has different summer dates. Tissington in Derbyshire decorates its five wells with collages using natural materials—pebbles, feathers, seeds—set in clay. Charming, but a far cry from the last recorded ceremony in 1350. Further north the decoration is coloured cloths hung on surrounding trees—regrettable litter though based on the genuine tradition that disease could be transferred from the patient to some symbol of him. For these waters were not merely water, precious enough, but medicine. For children, all wells are wishing wells, the water to be quaffed copiously and with abandon. The same childlike faith helped to effect the cure by a decoction in well water of fifty herbs taken fasting, while the rinsing with the water as much as its supposed properties soothed the eyes. Not for nothing was Naaman told to wash seven times in the Jordan!

WEDDING DAY

Although since the beginning of this century marriage has changed out of recognition, weddings have altered hardly at all. Couples who 'never darken a church door' will insist (to the chagrin of the parson) on going through the whole process—not altogether because it has been artificially popularised, nor because the reception will satisfactorily kill with one stone all the courtesies due to the birds who have given presents. ¶ No, let us admit that we all go sentimental over a wedding. We like dressing up, especially in lace and veil; we like the fairytale ritual of exchange of vows and ring, the pretty procession, the raising of glasses with 'beaded bubbles winking at the brim', the ceremonial cutting of the cake, a morsel of which under the pillow will make our dreams come true. ¶ A hundred years ago, when everyone knew everyone else and all attended church or chapel, a country wedding was genuinely a sacrament. The 'foreigner' bride (from the nearest village!) was welcomed into the community, and wedding was also marriage, by which each individual there traced the common ancestry back to Adam.

MIDSUMMER EVE

On St John's Eve in olden days girls would test their fates in love by harmless magic. At night two flowering stems of houseleek ('midsummer men') would be held firm in a crevice. If by morning they had wilted towards each other the love affair would prosper, if in opposite directions it was doomed. Here the speaker is imagined as Izz Huett, fellow-milkmaid with Tess of the d'Urbervilles, and, like all four of them, in love with Angel Clare.

Supperless, I've set upright
Midsummer men by full moon's light,
Bending together or apart
To give me hope—or break my heart.
One is myself, one Angel Clare.
That I, a dairy-maid, should dare!
Yet through that floodwater he carried
Me in his arms like bride new-married....

If this miscarries, I will weave
More magic come St. Agnes' Eve.

H.T.

FRIDAY

Our language still keeps the names of heathen gods for our days of the week, Roman or Germanic, derived from neither but from their remote common origin. In this country we commemorate the Norse mythology of the gods of Asgard. Friday is named after Frija or Freya, goddess of love, the root in our word 'friend'. In French she is Venus and her day 'vendredi'. One of those sky-scapes with high white stratus and rainladen cumulus below happened to form on a Friday:

Freya has spun her finest weft,
Across her sky loom stretched and barred
In sweeping strands, to keep below
The solid swollen vapours, left
Laden with earth-born rain and snow,
From the clear sapphire of Asgard.

H.T.

39

HAYSEL

Two verses from *Haymaking*

Where once the haycocks lay, soft-mounded and sweet,
Compounded was that hay of sorrel and cow-wheat,
Trefoil and tormentil, potentilla, meadowsweet,
Melilot and Storksbill pungent in June heat,
Lady's bedstraw, woodruff, lady's mantle, marguerite,
With marjoram flowers enough to make the air sweet,
Wagwants and nameless grasses, goosegrass, cocksfeet,
Feverfew and creeping Jenny, eyebright neat—

Now the stinking engine roars down streamlined fields;
Oblong haycocks its vomit yields.
Of sterile and purest ley, parcelled and hard,
Compounded is that hay, by no flowers marred.
Tested and scentless, weedless and clean,
Clinical bales litter the June scene.

R.T.

41

ST. SWITHIN'S DAY: July 15th

St. Swithin's day an ye do rain
For forty days it will remain.
St. Swithin's day an ye be fair
For forty days'twill rain nae mair.

Why should that Bishop of Winchester be held responsible for so often spoiling our summer holidays? He was a humble soul, insisting that he be buried not only outside the abbey church but on the north side, where feet might tread and roof drip on his grave. But in 971 A.D., more than a hundred years after his death, he was exhumed and re-buried with ceremony in the cathedral. ¶ The date was July 15th, about the time when a long spell of unusually wet or dry weather is liable to set in. Are there no other such patches in the calendar? Maybe, but this includes hay and corn harvest, and is watched apprehensively. Observation confirms it more often than not—so long as it is elastic: France gives a choice of two saints to start the forty days, on June 8th or June 19th, while Germany postpones them to July 27th. Another rhyme marks their end—

All the tears St. Swithin can cry,
St. Bartlemy's mantle wipes them dry.

St. Bartholomew's day is August 24th, and even the great drought of 1976, which made us all vow we would never again complain of rain, broke on August 29th.

43

LAMMAS: August 1st

Lammas, like Plough Monday, shows the desperate importance of bread in the 'good' old days. It was the loaf-mass, and the loaf-divider (hlafdige) of the household became our 'lady'. August 1st is an early date, the first fruits rather than the harvest. Did it become established between 1000 and 1300 A.D., when our climate was warmer, and vines flourished in fields as well as 'round the thatch eaves'? ¶ Every civilisation has always celebrated its own grain—wheat, oats, barley, rye, millet, maize, rice—with its own prayers and propitiations to god, or to bird on the corn stack! Today churches contrive to give pride of place to a sheaf of corn and, where there is a craftsman baker, a huge ornately plaited loaf, among the kindly fruits of the earth. Japanese farmers held a specially charming 'mass' on the day following their own festival: they would make rice dumplings as an offering to the souls of insects inadvertently trodden underfoot throughout the year. On the same day anything borrowed should be returned—a custom that could
well be revived!

45

AUTUMN EQUINOX

All night the wild northwest roared in the pines.
Passionate, it would storm the wood and strain
The creaking rowan trees; fiercely the rain
Streamed slantwise to the earth in ceaselsss lines.
The owl's cry was drowned by the wind's hate:
Triumphing in its mighty will, aloud
It mocked with fiendish laugh; the ebony shroud
Of solid darkness pressed down like a weight.

Till, yellow-white, the violated dawn
Stared through the leaden wrack, silent and numb,
Naked of leaves, stained, but without a tear
(After that night of tears) left for the morn;
After that night of moaning voices, dumb,
Seeing the inky mountains all too clear.

H.T.

47

BAKING DAY

'Pie like Mother makes.' How did she make her memorable confections? If her cottage had a bread oven beside the open fireplace, when the fire of red-hot sticks was raked out it would cook on residual heat, maybe for neighbours as well as the family. Later came iron grates with hobs and little ovens on either side, much too slow for bread but ideal for milk puddings and slab cake. Baking, as distinct from simmering in a pot over the fire, could not be a daily affair but must be set apart, the children banished till it was safely over, when they would be rewarded with tart or bun or, like Richard Jefferies' Amaryllis, with a corner of hot lardy cake. ¶ When Mother shaped her quartern loaves she would contrive that a little dough should be left over. This she treated as flaky pastry, rolling it into a rectangle, spreading two-thirds of it with dabs of home-clarified lard and scattering it liberally with currants and sugar. Then it was folded in three, turned sideways, re-rolled, re-folded twice, scored across the top, 'proved', and baked with the bread. Dough being reluctant to absorb much fat, the sweetened surplus sinks to the bottom of the tin and becomes that delectable foundation of soft toffee.

ALL SOULS' DAY: November 1st

With unguents and with spice did they suppose
Death slain? The gold sarcophagus arose
To immortality, corpse crumbled—and
If Tutankhamun lives nobody knows.

With ritual and obituary verse
Still we propitiate, fearing the worse:
And when has godless evolutionist
Rhapsodised by a belovéd hearse?

Only the pure in heart beheld the Grail.
With Death can we who deal in death prevail?
Death to man and beast, to earth and air?
Can the blood-blinded see beyond the veil?

H.T.

Here
lyeth e
Body of
Arin Wise
Died 1712.

BONFIRE DAY: November 5th

One would have thought that the nightly lurid skies and explosions of 1939-45 would have put paid forever to celebrating Guy Fawkes' Day. Not so! fire still has a fatal fascination, and he is a good excuse for the necessary task of burning the garden's accumulation of seeding grass, sodden weeds, gale-wrenched twigs and fallen leaves. A melancholy aspect: 'the whole year sets apace.' But the crackle and the curling blue smoke are cheering, while the ash will help to nourish new life next year.

The Burnt Shell

This shell came through the bonfire's heat
Still with its spiral markings: once
It ate to live, and lived to eat;
And shells from past millenia
Gleam in the stones beneath my feet.
What is 'dead', and what 'alive'?
What, of us mortals, will survive?

H.T.

STIR-UP SUNDAY

The collect for the last of the interminable Sundays after Trinity begins 'Stir up, O Lord, the wills of thy faithful people, that they, plenteously bringing forth the fruit of good works . . .' How it hits the nail on the head! Given the will, what good works might be plenteously brought forth! The housewife who has been vaguely thinking for some time that she should be doing something about Christmas is suddenly reminded of stirring up puddings.

A bag pudding the queen did make
And stuffed it full of plums,
And in it put great lumps of fat
As big as my two thumbs.

The other ingredients are ticked off the list as they go into the largest crock in the house. Everyone must stir, for luck. Someone holds the baby's fat little arm and guides the wooden spoon round. Then into the basins goes the rich mixture, redolent of spice, fruit and brandy, the fourpence-a-yard unbleached calico cloths securely tied, their four corners knotted to make a handle. The old copper's fire has been lighted as if for a washday, and when the water boils the puddings are gently lowered— for Christmas, for Twelfth Night, for the next birthday, and a fourth 'in case'. Four good hours a-cooking (with three more on the day), and Advent can be faced with that much clearer conscience.

55

CHRISTMAS DAY

Most grownups nowadays would be content with a Christmas once in ten years. Not so children: it is their festival—and not only, though maybe chiefly, for the presents! They enjoy an Occasion as only children can, so a special one has been devised for them. It seems that the Christingle originated in Denmark, spread thence to Germany, and was brought here by the Moravians. Theirs is a lighted candle set prettily in an orange with, for sconce, a goose quill cut into four strips, their ends weighted with sweets to make them curve over and bob as the holder moves in a solemn procession round the church. Instead of a split quill the Danes use four little kebab-like wooden sticks threaded with raisins and nuts —which like the orange itself cannot be eaten till the service is over, another adult device, like bobbing for apples, for spinning out the Christmas fare! ¶ Ingle, as in 'inglenook', refers to the fire (ignis) on the hearth, sacred source of light as well as of warmth in the days before central heating, and symbol of family and home 'as we sat in a flock by the embers in hearthside ease', says Hardy, waiting for the oxen to kneel at midnight on Christmas Eve.

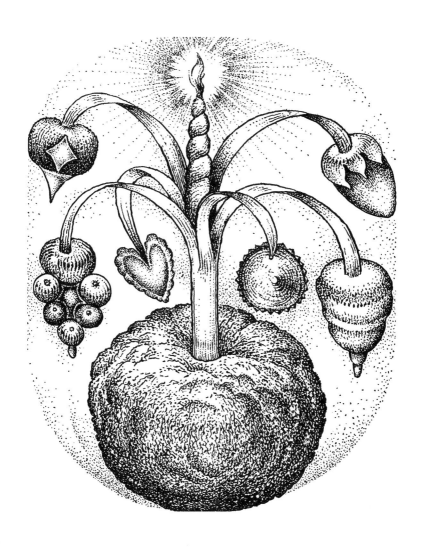

FINIS: Night

As day ends in night, so this Book of Days closes with a nocturne.

> Behind the sombre castellated tower
>   The unseen moon floods with a mellow light
> The hamlet lulled in sleep: it is the hour
>   When autumn dews invade the summer night.
>   And now, above the church, the crescent white
> Transforms the sable thatch to softer brown,
>   And in the misty valley, orange-bright,
> Facing the shadowy outline of the down,
> Twinkle the fallen-star lights of the distant town.

H.T.

from
The Old Stile Press

This book was first published
in a hand-printed edition limited to 200
signed & numbered copies
with 26 specially bound copies lettered A-Z,
in July 1986
by Frances & Nicolas McDowall at
The Old Stile Press, Catchmays Court,
Llandogo, Nr Monmouth, Gwent NP5 4TN.

¶ Details of Old Stile Press editions
can be obtained from
this address.

¶